BIG
ENGLISH 1

Mario Herrera • Christopher Sol Cruz

Contents

1. **Good Morning, Class!** 2
2. **My Family** 14
3. **My Body** 26

   Checkpoint Units 1–3 38

4. **My Favorite Clothes** 42
5. **Busy at Home** 54
6. **On the Farm** 66

   Checkpoint Units 4–6 78

7. **Party Time** 82
8. **Fun and Games** 94
9. **Play Time** 106

   Checkpoint Units 7–9 118

Checkpoint Cutouts 123

YLE Practice Materials 129

Stickers

BIG ENGLISH
♪ Song ♪

From the mountaintops to the bottom of the sea,
From a big blue whale to a baby bumblebee—
If you're big, if you're small, you can have it all,
And you can be anything you want to be!

It's bigger than you. It's bigger than me.
There's so much to do, and there's so much to see!
The world is big and beautiful, and so are we!
Think big! Dream big! Big English!

So in every land, from the desert to the sea,
We can all join hands and be one big family.
If we love, if we care, we can go anywhere!
The world belongs to everyone; it's ours to share.

It's bigger than you. It's bigger than me.
There's so much to do, and there's so much to see!
The world is big and beautiful, and so are we!
Think big! Dream big! Big English!

It's bigger than you. It's bigger than me.
There's so much to do, and there's so much to see!
The world is big and beautiful and waiting for me . . .
    a one, two, three . . .
Think big! Dream big! Big English!

Unit 1

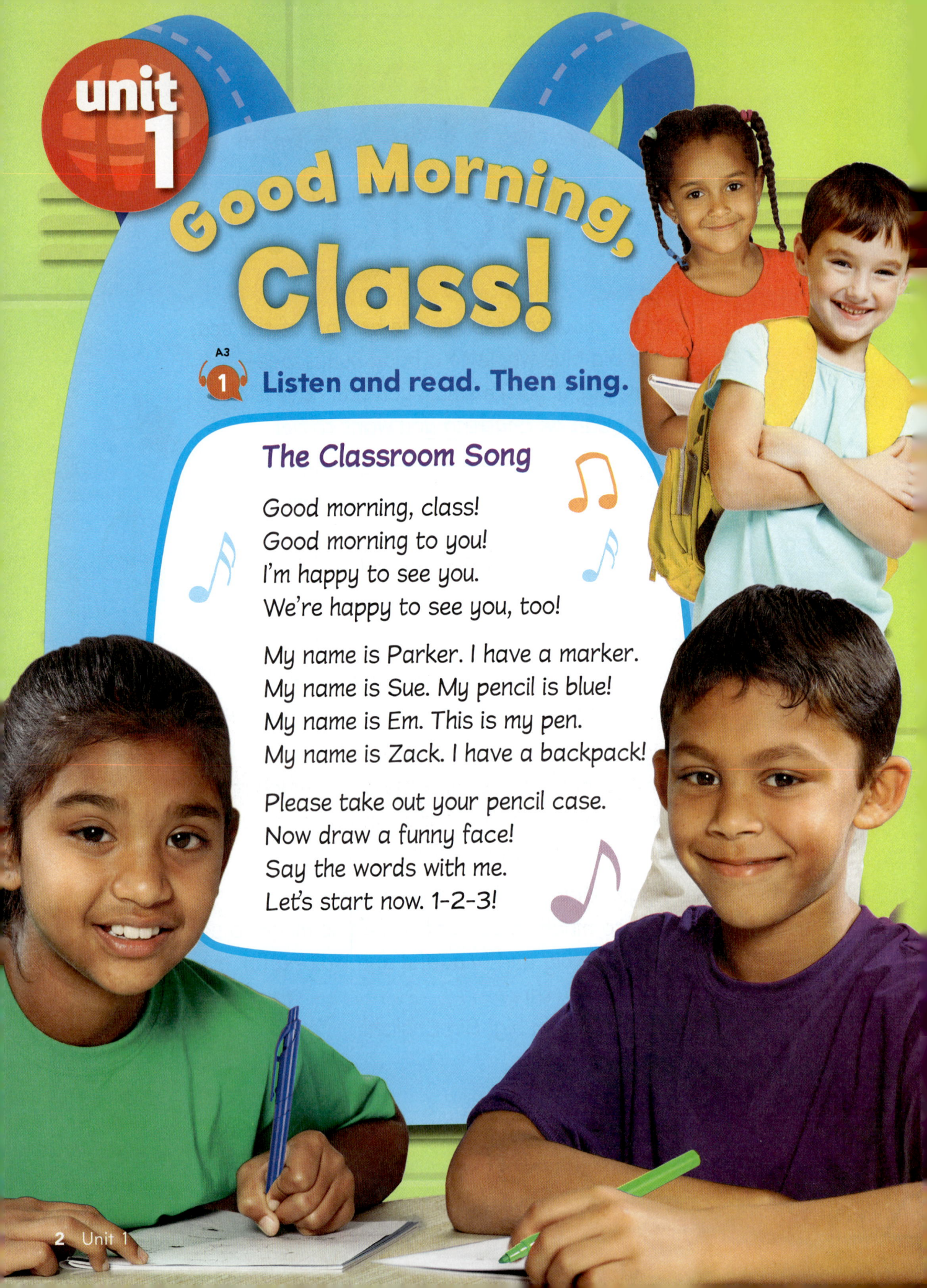

Good Morning, Class!

1 Listen and read. Then sing.

The Classroom Song

Good morning, class!
Good morning to you!
I'm happy to see you.
We're happy to see you, too!

My name is Parker. I have a marker.
My name is Sue. My pencil is blue!
My name is Em. This is my pen.
My name is Zack. I have a backpack!

Please take out your pencil case.
Now draw a funny face!
Say the words with me.
Let's start now. 1-2-3!

2 Listen. Point and say.

1. backpack
2. book
3. chair
4. crayon
5. desk
6. eraser
7. marker
8. pen
9. pencil
10. ruler

3 Listen. Point and say.

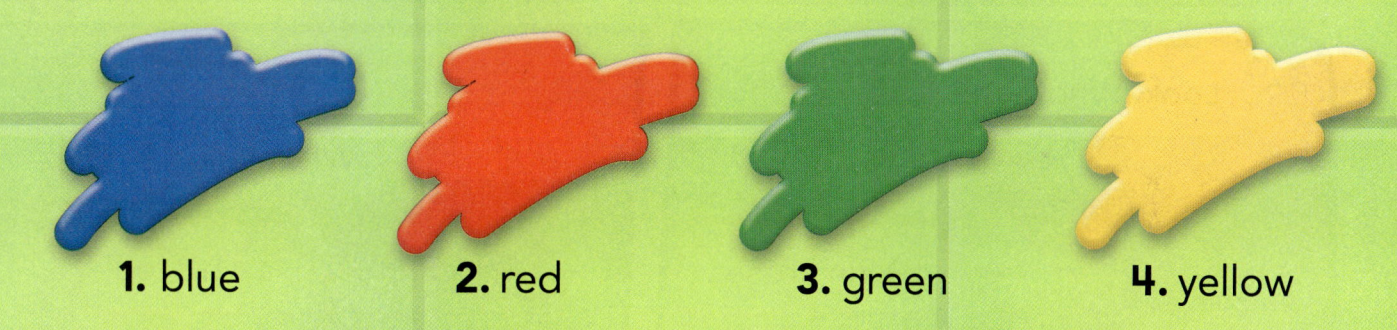

1. blue
2. red
3. green
4. yellow

4 Look at 3. Listen. Ask and answer with a partner.

What color is it?

It's blue.

Unit 1 3

Story

5 Listen to the story.

Classroom Colors

1.
- Look, Jeremy. What's this?
- It's a marker.

2.
- Good! What color is it?
- It's red.
- Yes, Jeremy. It's red.

3.
- Look. What's this?
- It's an eraser.

4.
- Yes, good! What color is it?
- It's red!

Red? No, Jeremy. It's green.

No! Look. It's red!

5

6

6 Look at the story. Color.

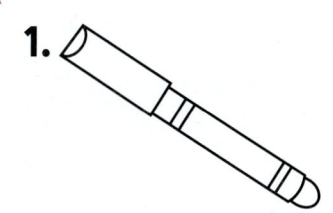

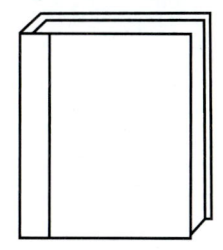

1.
2.
3.
4.

7 Draw two things in your classroom. Color them red, green, blue, or yellow.

8 THINK BIG What other things are red, green, blue, or yellow?

Unit 1 5

Language in Action

9 **Listen and say.**

Linda: Hi! What's your name?
Bobby: My name is Bobby.
Linda: What's this?
Bobby: It's a pencil.

10 **Work with a partner. Look at 9. Role-play.**

11 **Listen. Stick.**

1. 
2. 
3. 
4.

6 Unit 1

Grammar

What's this?   It's a chair.

It is = It's
What is = What's

12 **Listen and circle.** (A10)

1.

2.

3.

4.

13 **Work with a partner. Look at 12. Ask and answer.**

What's this?

It's an eraser.

What color is it?

It's red.

Unit 1 7

Connections | Content: Math

14 Listen and trace. Point and say.

1	2	3	4	5
one	two	three	four	five
6	7	8	9	10
six	seven	eight	nine	ten

15 Listen. Count and color.

Around the World | Connections

16 Look. Listen and match.

In Our Classrooms

1 Luis
2 Ahmed
3 Masako

a. b. c.

17 Draw your classroom objects.

18 Work with a partner. Look at **17**. Ask and answer.

What's this?

It's a pencil.

Unit 1 9

Sounds and Letters | The Alphabet

19 Listen and point. Say.

A B C D E F G H I
J K L M N O P Q R
S T U V W X Y Z

20 Listen and point. Then sing.

a b c d e f g h i
j k l m n o p q r
s t u v w x y z

21 Write.

What's your name?

My name is _____.

22 Spell your name.

Spell your name, please.

L-U-I-S-A.

Be polite. | **Values in Action**

23 Look and listen. Point to the picture.

Thank you.
You're welcome.
Please sit down.
Thank you.

24 Look at 23. Role-play with a partner.

PROJECT

25 Make a Be Polite poster.

Be Polite!
Thank you. You're welcome.

Unit 1 11

Review | Listening and Speaking

26 **Work in a small group. Look, listen, and say.**

"I spy . . . something blue!"

"It's a chair."

"No, it isn't."

"It's a book."

"Yes, it is."

27 **Play *I Spy . . .* with the whole class.**

Vocabulary and Grammar | Review

28 **Listen. Look and match.**

1. It's an eraser.

2. It's a book.

3. It's a desk.

4. It's a crayon.

5. It's a chair.

a. 
b.
c. 
d.
e.

29 **Listen and circle.**

1.  
2.  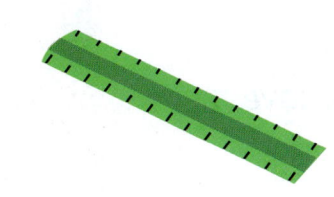
3.

I Can
- ☐ name classroom objects.
- ☐ count to ten.
- ☐ identify colors.

Unit 1   13

unit 2 My Family

1 Listen and read. Then sing.

I Love My Family

My family, my family!
I love my family.
See them in this picture.
They mean so much to me.

My father, my mother!
My sister, my brother!
We have so much fun.
They're number one.

My family, my family!
I love my family.
I love them and they love me,
That's why we're family!

2 Listen. Point and say.

- father
- mother
- grandfather
- grandmother
- brother
- sister
- Lisa

3 Draw your family.

4 Look at 3. Listen. Ask and answer with a partner.

Who's he?

He's my grandfather.

Unit 2   15

Story

5 Listen to the story.

A Big Family

1
- Is this your photo album, Fran?
- Yes! These are pictures of my family.

2
- Who are they?
- That's my father and mother.

3
- How many brothers do you have?
- I have three brothers—Stan, Dan, and Van.

4
- And who are they?
- They're my sisters—Jan and Nan.

5	6
Who's she? / She's my baby sister.	What's her name? / Ann!

6 Listen and circle.

1.  
2.  
3.  
4.

7 Draw Fran's family.

Unit 2

Language in Action

8 Listen and say.

Pam: Who are they?
John: She's my sister and he's my brother.
Pam: How many brothers and sisters do you have?
John: I have one sister and two brothers.

9 Work with a partner. Look at 8. Role-play.

10 Listen. Stick.

1. 
2. 
3. 
4.

18   Unit 2

Grammar

How many brothers and sisters **do** you **have**?   I **have** one brother.
I **have** two sisters.

11 Listen and circle.

1.
2. 
3.
4.

12 Work with a partner. Ask and answer about your family.

How many brothers and sisters do you have?

I have two sisters.

Unit 2   19

Connections | **Content: Social Studies**

13 Look and listen. Write the number.

14 Draw an animal family. Talk with a partner.

I see a mother and a baby.

15 Can you name two other baby animals?

20 Unit 2

Around the World | **Connections**

16 Look and listen.

Popular Names

1. Maria
2. Minjoon
3. Celine

17 Make a name tag. Cut and wear.

Luis

18 Ask and answer. Count the names in your class.

Name	How many?
Maria	3
Juan	4
Isabella	2
Miguel	1

Unit 2   21

Sounds and Letters | Letters *b* and *p*

19 **Listen and point. Say.**

1. **b**aby
2. **b**ook
3. **p**encil
4. **p**arents

20 **Listen. Write *b* or *p*.**

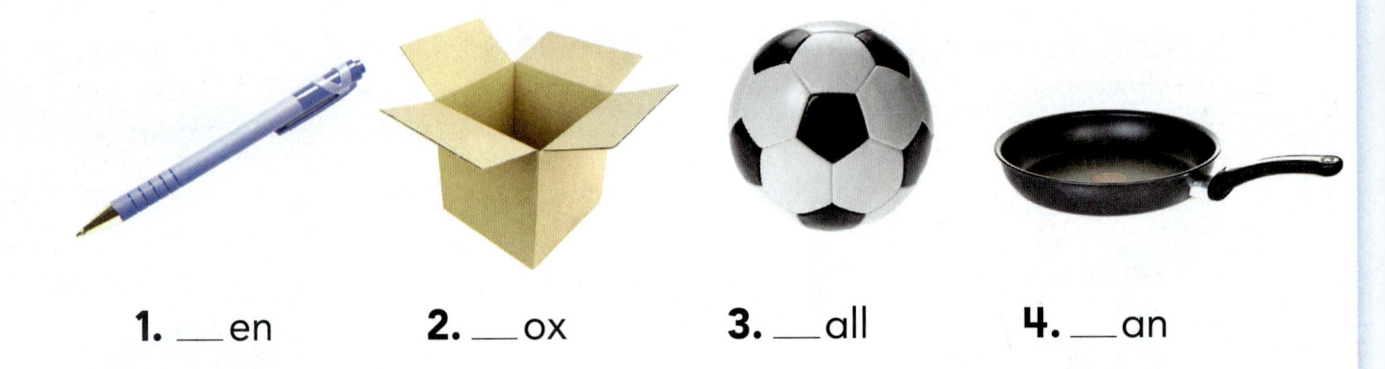

1. __en
2. __ox
3. __all
4. __an

21 **Listen and say. Underline *b* and *p*.**

1. It's a <u>b</u>lue <u>p</u>en.
2. Pedro is my baby brother.
3. Ben and Patti have big backpacks.
4. My parents are Felipe and Anna.

22 Unit 2

Help your family. | Values in Action

22 **Listen. Circle.**

"Can I help you?"

"Yes, thank you."

1. Pam helps her **brother / sister**.

"Please help me."

"OK. I can help you."

2. Tommy helps his **brother / sister**.

23 **Look at 22. Role-play with a partner.**

PROJECT

24 **Make an I Can Help poster.**

I Can Help!

Unit 2 23

Review | Listening and Speaking

25 **Work with a partner. Ask and answer. Draw your partner's family.**

Who's in your family?

My mother, my father, my two sisters, and my brother.

24　Unit 2

Vocabulary and Grammar | Review

26 Listen and check (✓).

1.
2.
3.
4.

27 Listen. Write the number.

I Can
☐ talk about my family.
☐ say how many brothers and sisters I have.

Unit 2   25

unit 3
My Body

1 Listen and read. Then sing.

My Body Song

With my ears I hear.
With my eyes I see.
With my mouth I sing.
Sing along with me!

I have ten fingers.
I have ten toes.
Two arms and two legs
But just one nose!

I wave my hands in the air.
I run my fingers through my hair.
I make a silly face and then
I sing my body song, my body song,
I sing my body song again!

2 Listen. Point and say.

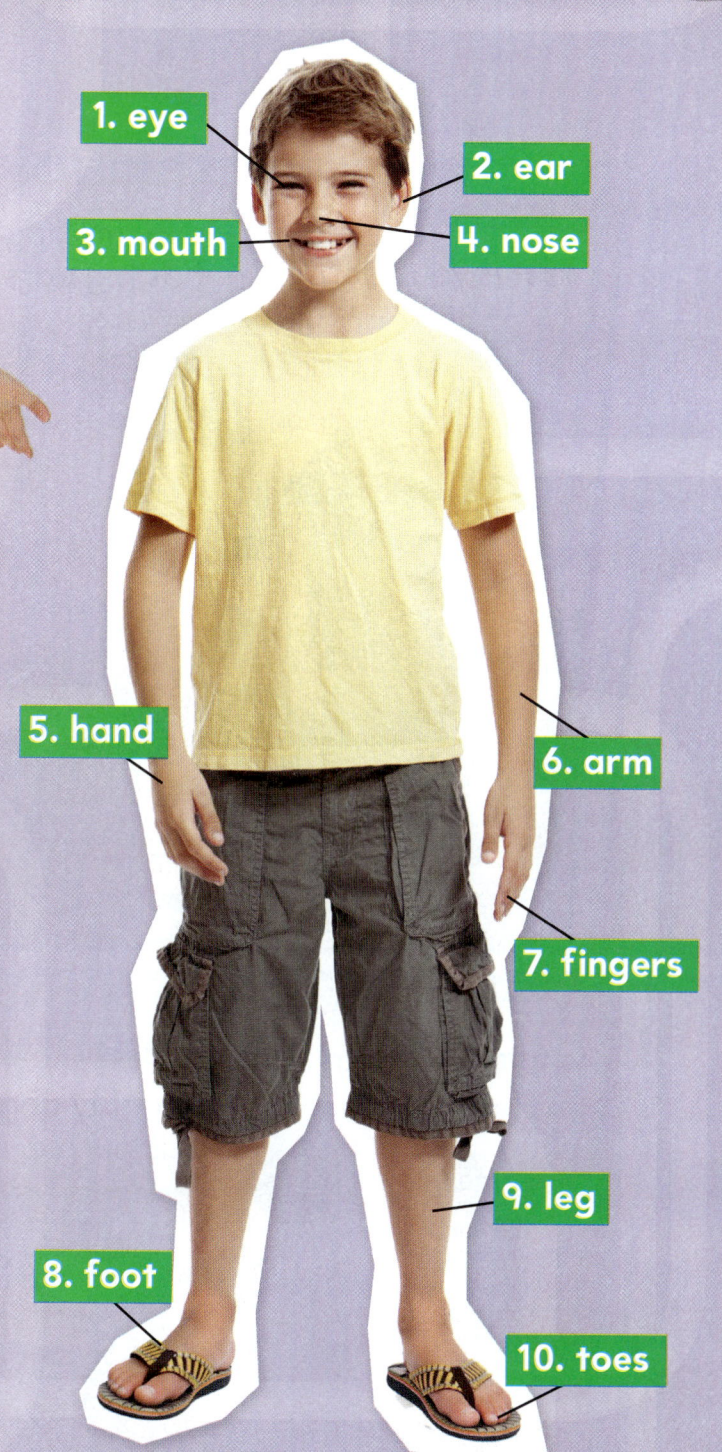

1. eye
2. ear
3. mouth
4. nose
5. hand
6. arm
7. fingers
8. foot
9. leg
10. toes

3 Listen. Point and say.

1. I have two ears. 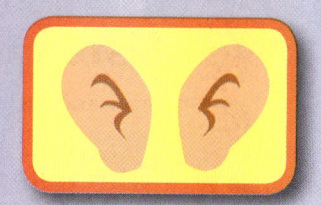
2. I have one mouth. 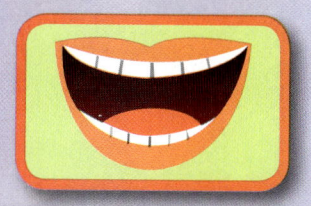
3. I have ten fingers. 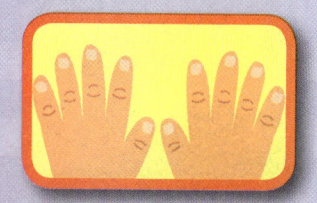
4. I have two feet. 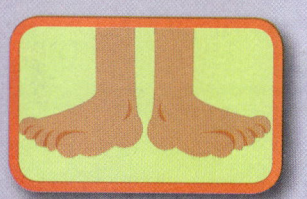
5. I have two hands. 
6. I have ten toes.

4 Look at 3. Listen. Ask and answer with a partner.

How many ears does he have?

He has two ears.

Unit 3 27

Story

5 Listen to the story.

Lost Dog!

1
Do you have my dog?
I don't know. Let's see.

2
Is this your dog?
No, my dog has big ears.

3
Is this your dog?
No, my dog has short legs.

4
Is this your dog?
No. My dog is purple.

Purple? Oh! Does it have big ears?

Yes, it does.

5

Aha! A toy dog!

Yes! That's my dog! Thank you.

6

6 Listen and circle.

1.
2.
3.

7 Draw the boy's dog.

Unit 3

Language in Action

8. Listen and say.

Alex: Wow. That's a cool dinosaur!
Mia: I know. It has a small head and a long neck.
Alex: Does it have long legs?
Mia: No, it doesn't. It has short legs.

9. Work with a partner. Look at 8. Role-play.

10. Look and listen. Stick.

1. It has a small head.
2. It has a big head.
3. It has short arms.
4. It has long legs.

Grammar

Does she **have** long hair?	Yes, she **does**.
Does he **have** short hair?	No, he **doesn't**.
Does it **have** a small head?	Yes, it **does**.
Does it **have** a big head?	No, it **doesn't**.

11 Listen and check (✔).

1.

2.

3.

4.

12 Work with a partner. Ask and answer about your family and pets.

Does your sister have long hair?

No, she doesn't. She has short hair.

Unit 3   31

Connections | Content: Science

13 **Look. Listen and say.**

1. see
2. smell
3. taste
4. hear

14 **Listen. Match and say.**

1. I see with my ____. 
2. I taste with my ____. 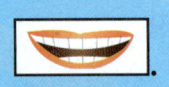
3. I hear with my ____. 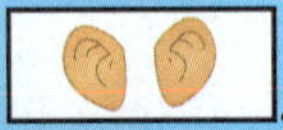
4. I smell with my ____.

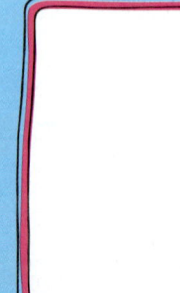

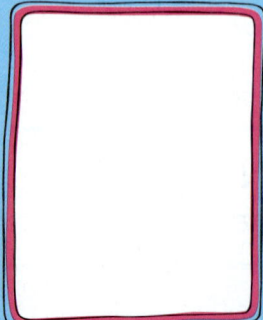

a. 
b. 
c. 
d.

15 **Draw and say.**

1. I see
2. I smell
3. I taste
4. I hear

Around the World | Connections

16 Look. Listen, point, and say.

Flags of All Colors

1. yellow
2. orange
3. purple
4. black
5. white
6. brown

17 Look and listen. Write the number.

Ireland    Brazil    South Africa

18 Draw and color your country's flag.

19 Look at 18. Talk with a partner.

What color is it?

It is red, white, and blue.

20 THINK BIG — How many colors does your flag have?

Unit 3 33

Sounds and Letters | Letters *d* and *t*

21 **Listen and point. Say.**

1. **d**esk
2. re**d**
3. **t**oes
4. foo**t**

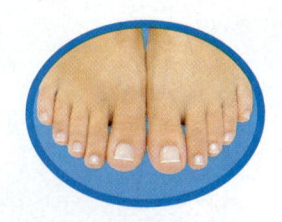

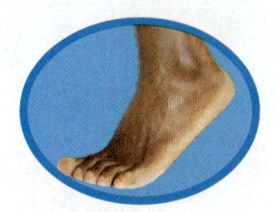

22 **Listen. Write *d* or *t*.**

1. __en
2. __og 
3. ba__
4. han__ 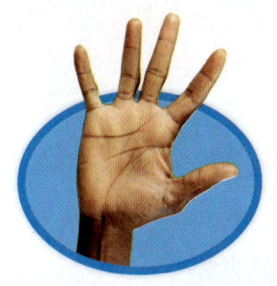

23 **Listen and say. Underline *d* and *t*.**

1. Does Dad have short hair?
2. Ted has two sisters.
3. Do Tim and Deb have red hair?
4. Dan sees a little white dog under the table.

Keep clean. | **Values in Action**

24 Listen. Trace.

1. Wash
2. Rinse
3. Dry

25 Listen and sing.

Keep Clean

Every day
Before I eat
And after I play,
I wash my hands.

With water and soap
It's easy, you see.
You rub your hands
Just like me.

When you wash,
Sing this song.
Keep your hands clean
All day long!

PROJECT

26 Decorate a **Tissue Box.**

1. Cut out shapes.
2. Paste shapes.
3. Use a tissue.

Unit 3 35

Review | Listening and Speaking

27 Complete the monster. Listen and color.

28 Draw your own monster. Ask and answer with a partner.

How many legs does it have?

It has three legs.

Vocabulary and Grammar | Review

29 Listen and check (✓).

1. 
2. 
3. 
4.

30 Look and write.

| ear eye mouth nose |

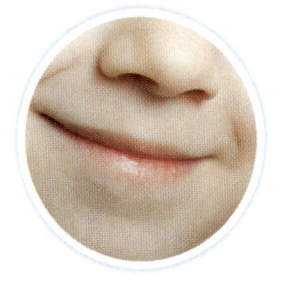

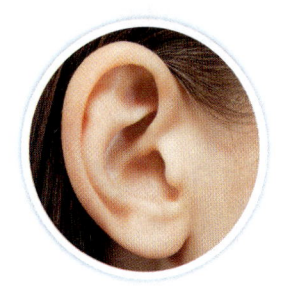

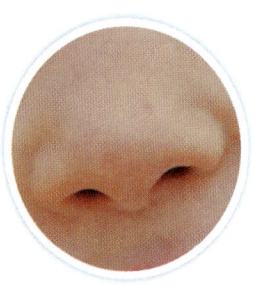

1. _____ 2. _____ 3. _____ 4. _____

I Can
☐ name parts of the body.
☐ talk about people and pets.

Unit 3 37

Checkpoint | Units 1–3

Do I Know It?

1 **Look and circle. Practice.**

😊 I know this.   😟 I don't know this.

1. p. 3

2. pp. 3, 33

3. p. 8

4. p. 15

5. eye, ear, mouth, nose, hand, arm, fingers, foot, leg, toes — p. 27

6. p. 30

Have students review the key language. Go to the pages indicated in each box.

I Can Do It!

2 **Get ready.** A56–57

A. Listen and number.

B. Look at **A** and point. Ask and answer.

- What's this?
- It's a backpack.

C. Listen and circle.

1. Ted

2. Kate

D. Look at **C** and point. Ask and answer.

- Who's she?
- She's Kate's sister.

Checkpoint Units 1–3

Checkpoint | Units 1–3

3 Get set.

✂ Cut out the cards on page 123.
Now you're ready to **Go!**

4 Go! A58

A. Listen. Put the cards on the numbers.

1	2	3
4	5	6

B. Point to a card. Ask and answer with a partner.

> Card 2. Does she have long hair?

> Yes, she does.

40 Checkpoint Units 1–3

5 Write or draw.

All About Me

My name is
_____.

This is me.

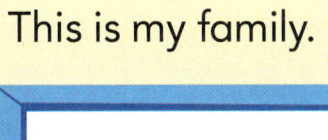

This is my family.

Do I Know It Now?

6 Think about it.

A. Go to page 38. Look and circle again.

B. Check (✔).

☐ I can start the next unit.

☐ I can ask my teacher for help and then start the next unit.

☐ I can practice and then start the next unit.

7 Rate this Checkpoint. Color the stars.

☆ easy   ☆ hard | ☆ fun   ☆ not fun

Checkpoint Units 1–3   41

Unit 4: My Favorite Clothes

1 Listen and read. Then chant.

These Are the Clothes

These are the clothes:
Shirts, pants, shoes.
These are the clothes
That we choose.

This is the skirt
I'll wear today.
This is the shirt
I'll wear to play.

These are the pants
I'll wear to school.
These are the pants
That look so cool.

These are the shoes
I like the best.
These are the shoes
That'll pass the test.

2 Listen. Point and say.

1. boots
2. dress
3. gloves
4. hat
5. jacket
6. pants
7. blouse
8. shoes
9. skirt
10. shirt

3 Listen and say. Write.

1. She's wearing a _____.

2. He's wearing _____.

3. She's wearing a _____.

4. He's wearing _____.

4 Look at 3. Listen. Point, ask, and answer.

What's she wearing?

She's wearing a red shirt.

Story

5 Listen to the story.

My Favorite Hat!

1. What are you wearing?

2. I'm wearing a green hat. It's my favorite hat.

3. What's she wearing? She's wearing an orange hat. It's her favorite hat.

4. What's she wearing? She's wearing a purple hat. It's her favorite hat.

5 — What are you wearing, Tommy?

6 — I'm wearing a funny hat. It's my favorite hat!

6 Look and match.

1. 
2. 
3. 
4.

a. 
b. 
c. 
d.

7 Draw your favorite hat from the story.

Language in Action

8 **Listen and say.**

Olivia: What's your brother wearing?
Mario: He's wearing a red shirt.
Olivia: His shirt is big.
Mario: Hey! That's not his shirt. That's my shirt!

9 **Work with a partner. Look at 8. Role-play.**

10 **Listen. Stick.**

big

small

new

old

46 Unit 4

Grammar

> What **are** you **wearing**?   **I'm wearing** a green hat.
> What**'s** he/she **wearing**?   He**'s**/She**'s wearing** white pants.

11 Listen and match.

1.    2.    3.    4.

a.    b.    c.    d.

12 Work with a partner. Ask and answer about your clothes.

What are you wearing?

I'm wearing an orange shirt and blue pants.

Unit 4   **47**

Connections | **Content: Social Studies**

13 Look. Listen and say. Trace.

1. It's ___cold___ in the ___mountains___.

2. It's ___hot___ in the ___desert___.

3. It's ___wet___ in the ___jungle___.

14 Listen. Look and match.

15 Draw clothes for the weather. Ask your partner to guess *hot*, *cold*, or *wet*.

48 Unit 4

Around the World | Connections

16 Look and listen. Write. England

Funny Hats!

flowers   birds   horses

1. Her hat has _____ on it.
2. Her hat has _____ on it.
3. Her hat has _____ on it.

17 Color the hat. Talk with a partner.

My hat has dogs on it.

What a funny hat!

18 THINK BIG When do you wear a funny hat? Tell a friend.

Unit 4 49

Sounds and Letters | Letters c and g

19 Listen and point. Say.

1. **c**at
2. **c**orn
3. **g**ame
4. do**g**

20 Listen. Write c or g.

1. ___ap
2. ___irl
3. fla___
4. ___ar

21 Listen and say. Underline c and g.

1. The cat got my big cookie!
2. Give my good friend a cup of cocoa.
3. The dog goes in the car with the girl.
4. Go see the cute goat in the grass.

Respect all cultures. | **Values in Action**

22 Look and listen.

1. Guatemala
2. Philippines
3. Kenya

23 Look at 22. Talk with a partner.

What are they wearing?

They're wearing traditional clothes from Guatemala.

PROJECT

24 Make a Traditional Clothes collage.

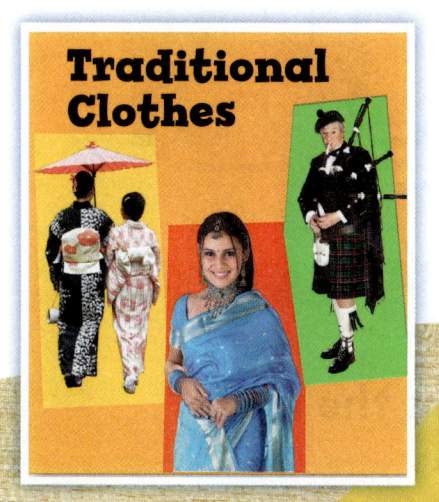

Unit 4 51

Review | Listening and Speaking

25 **Work in two pairs. Ask and answer.**

What's Valerie wearing?

She's wearing a green blouse and brown pants.

What's Mike wearing?

He's wearing a blue jacket and black pants.

26 **Work in two groups. One group looks away and answers the teacher. Score 1 point for each correct answer.**

What's Antonio wearing?

He's wearing a yellow shirt and blue pants.

Take turns. Which group remembers the most?

2 Listen. Point and say.

1. bathroom
2. bedroom
3. kitchen
4. dining room
5. living room

3 Listen and find in **2**. Point and say.

1. He's eating.
2. She's taking a bath.
3. He's reading.

4 Look at **3**. Listen. Ask and answer with a partner.

What's he doing?

He's eating.

Unit 5

Story

5 Listen to the story.

Fun at Home

1
— What are you doing, boys?
— We're playing.

2
— Where are you, Mom?
— I'm in the living room.

3
— What are you and Patrick doing?
— I'm reading and he's reading, too.
— That's good!

4
— Boys, I'm making lunch.

5

It's time for lunch! What are you doing now?

I'm drawing.

6

Patrick! What are *you* doing?

I'm drawing, too!

6 **Look at the story. Circle.**

1. Who is playing?

2. Who is making lunch?

3. Who is drawing?

7 **Draw your favorite character.**

8 **THINK BIG** **Tell why you like your favorite character.**

Language in Action

9 **Listen and say.**

Mrs. Miller: Hi, Grace.
Grace: Hi, Mrs. Miller. Where's Andrea?
Mrs. Miller: She's in the living room.
Grace: What's she doing?
Mrs. Miller: She's doing her homework.

10 **Work with a partner. Look at 9. Role-play.**

11 **Listen and stick.**

58 Unit 5

Grammar

Where's Dylan? — He**'s** in the dining room.
Where's Pam? — She**'s** in the living room.
Where are you? — I**'m** in the bedroom.

where is = where's
he is = he's
she is = she's
I am = I'm

12 **Listen and check (✔).**

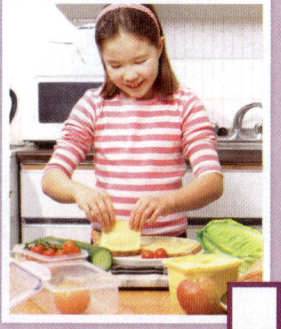

1. Where's Sara?

2. Where's Manny?

3. Where's Kevin?

4. Where's Peggy?

13 **Work with a partner. Look at 12. Ask and answer.**

Where's Sara?

She's in the kitchen.

Connections | Content: Art

14 Look. Listen and say.

1. square
2. circle
3. triangle
4. rectangle

15 Look and listen. Write the number.

16 Draw shapes. Color. Write how many.

_____ squares

_____ circles

_____ triangles

_____ rectangles

60 Unit 5

Around the World | **Connections**

17 Look and listen.

Homes

1. apartment
2. yurt
3. houseboat
4. lighthouse

18 Draw your home. Talk with a partner.

My home is square.

My home is old.

my home

Unit 5 61

Sounds and Letters | Short *a* Sound

19 **Listen and point. Say.**

1. sn**a**ck
2. b**a**sketball
3. D**a**d
4. c**a**t

20 **Listen and write. Use the words from 19.**

1. Mom is eating a _____ in the bedroom.

2. Grandpa is giving our white _____ a bath in the living room.

3. Grandma is playing _____ in the dining room.

4. _____ is sleeping in the kitchen. What a funny family!

21 **Listen and say. Underline *a*.**

1. The c<u>a</u>t is sitting on my j<u>a</u>cket.

2. Sam and Manny have big hands.

3. Patti's backpack is in the bathroom.

4. Dad is at home with my grandmother.

Help at home. | **Values in Action**

22 Listen and write.

1. What's he doing?
   He's _____.

2. What's she doing?
   She's _____ the dishes.

23 How do you help at home? Act it out. Your partner guesses.

He's drying the dishes.

PROJECT

24 Make a **Helping at Home** chart. Work in small groups.

	Me	1_____	2_____	3_____
Clean my room.				
Do my homework.				
Help my parents.				
Wash the dishes.				

Unit 5

Review | Listening and Speaking

25 Work in groups. Play a memory game.

Student 1: Act and say.

"I'm eating lunch."

Student 2: Talk about Student 1. Then act and say.

"She's eating lunch. I'm reading a book."

"She's eating lunch. He's reading a book. I'm washing my face."

Student 3: Talk about Students 1 and 2. Then act and say.

Play with the whole class. How much can you remember?

64 Unit 5

Vocabulary and Grammar | Review

26 Listen and number.

27 Look and write.

drawing   playing   reading   talking

1. She's _____.
2. He's _____. 
3. He's _____. 
4. She's _____. 

I Can
- ☐ name rooms in a house.
- ☐ talk about daily activities.

Unit 5 65

Unit 6
On the Farm

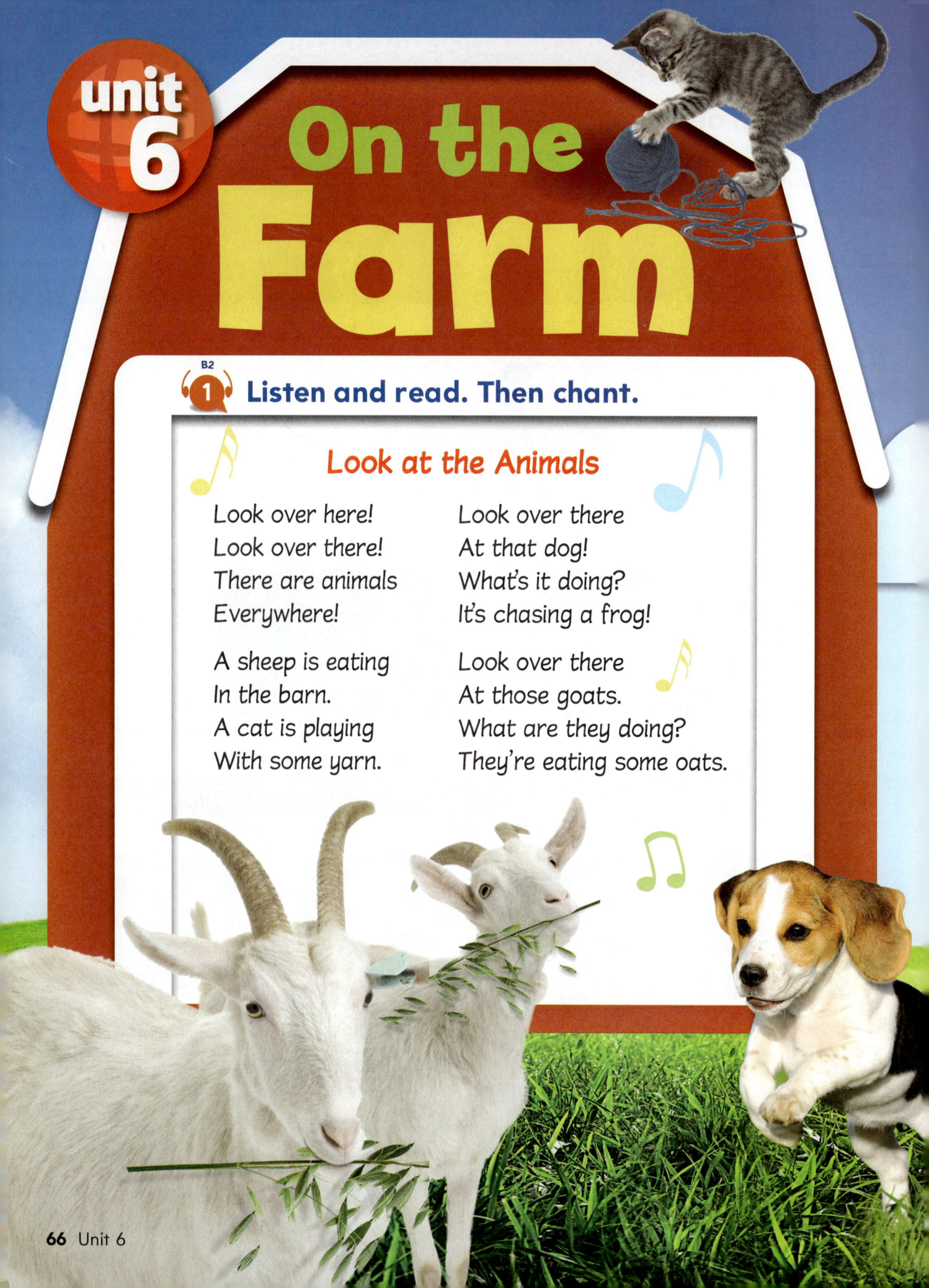

1 Listen and read. Then chant.

Look at the Animals

Look over here!
Look over there!
There are animals
Everywhere!

A sheep is eating
In the barn.
A cat is playing
With some yarn.

Look over there
At that dog!
What's it doing?
It's chasing a frog!

Look over there
At those goats.
What are they doing?
They're eating some oats.

2. Listen. Point and say.

1. cat
2. dog 
3. cow 
4. sheep 
5. turtle 
6. horse 
7. duck 
8. frog 
9. hen 
10. goat 

3. Listen and say.

1. It's jumping.
2. It's sleeping. 
3. It's running. 
4. It's eating. 
5. It's swimming. 
6. It's flying. 

4. Look at 3. Listen. Ask and answer with a partner.

What is it?

It's a frog.

What's it doing?

It's jumping.

Story

5 **Listen to the story.**

Lunch Time!

1
- Is that your horse?
- Yes, it is.

2
- What's it doing?
- It's eating an apple.

3
- What's the goat eating?
- It's eating hay.

4
- What are the hens eating?
- They're eating worms and bugs.

Worms and bugs? Oh, no!

Are you ready for lunch?

Yes. But no worms and bugs, please!

5

6

6 **Look and match.**

1. 
2. 
3. 
4.

a. 
b. 
c. 
d.

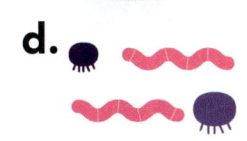

7 **Draw your favorite lunch.**

Unit 6 **69**

Language in Action

8 **Listen and say.**

Peggy: What's the sheep doing?
Matt: It's chasing the chicks.
Peggy: What are the chicks doing?
Matt: They're running!

9 **Work with a partner. Look at 8. Role-play.**

10 **Listen. Stick.**

Grammar

What's the duck doing?	It's swimming.
What are the cows doing?	They're eating.
What's he/she doing?	He's/She's running.

11 Listen and check (✔).

1.

2.

3.

4.

12 Look at **11**. Ask and answer with a partner.

What are the horses doing?

They're eating hay.

Unit 6

Connections | **Content: Social Studies**

13 Look at the baby animals. Listen and say.

1. It's a chick.
2. It's a puppy. 
3. It's a kitten. 

14 Listen. Look and match.

1. 
2.  
3.

a.
b.
c.

72 Unit 6

Around the World | **Connections**

15 Look and listen. Match.

Pets

1. Australia
2. Japan
3. United States

a. beetle
b. wallaby
c. skunk

16 Draw your favorite pet.

Unit 6 73

Sounds and Letters | Short *e* Sound

17 **Listen and point. Say.**

1. p**e**ts
2. h**e**n
3. n**e**st
4. **e**ggs

18 **Listen and write. Use the words from 17. Say.**

1. My family lives on a farm. I have many _____.

2. My favorite pet is Penny. She's a _____.

3. Penny sits on a _____ in the hen house.

4. We love Penny! She gives us _____.

19 **Listen and say. Underline *e*.**

1. Emma has a red dress.
2. Eric has two pencils and a pen on his desk.
3. Ben is getting dressed in the bedroom.
4. Ted is talking to ten men.

Be kind to animals. | **Values in Action**

20 **Listen. Find and number.**

feeding    walking    brushing    playing

21 **Look at 20. Role-play with a partner.**

What are you doing?

I'm feeding the birds.

22 **THINK BIG** **How are you kind to animals? Draw a picture.**

PROJECT

23 **Make a Bird Feeder.**

1. Clean.    2. Cut.    3. Tie.    4. Fill.    5. Hang.

Unit 6 75

Review | Listening and Speaking

24 Listen, point, and say. Then act out.

1.
2.
3.
4.
5.
6.

25 Work in teams. Act out. Ask and answer.

What are they doing?

They're jumping.

76 Unit 6

Vocabulary and Grammar | Review

26 **Look and write.**

1. They're _____.
2. It's _____. 
3. They're _____. 
4. It's _____. 
5. It's _____. 
6. It's _____. 

eating
flying
jumping
running
sleeping
swimming

27 **Look and write.**

duck   frog   hen   sheep

1. _____
2. _____ 
3. _____ 
4. _____

I Can
☐ name animals.
☐ talk about what animals and people are doing.

Checkpoint | Units 4–6

Do I Know It?

1. **Look and circle. Practice.**

   😊 I know this.   😟 I don't know this.

1. p. 43	2. p. 43
3. p. 55	4. p. 55
5. p. 67	6. p. 67

   Have students review the key language. Go to the pages indicated in each box.

78 Checkpoint Units 4–6

I Can Do It!

2 Get ready.

A. Look. Circle the correct word.

1. The mother is in the **dining room / bathroom**.
2. The father is in the **kitchen / bedroom**.
3. The girl is in the **bedroom / living room**.

B. Look at **A** and point. Ask and answer.

> What's she wearing?

> She's wearing a green shirt and brown pants.

C. Listen and number.

Checkpoint | Units 4–6

3 **Get set.**

STEP 1 Cut out the cards on page 125.

STEP 2 Put the cards on your desk. Mix the cards up. Now you're ready to **Go!**

4 **Go!**

A. Arrange the cards to make the person below. Ask and answer with a partner.

- Where is she?
- What's she wearing?
- What's she doing?

B. Make 3 more people. Don't show your cards. Describe one of your people. Your partner makes the same person. Show your cards and check.

> He's in the bathroom. He's feeding the bird. . .

5 **Write or draw.**

All About Me

My favorite animal is
_____.

I'm wearing
_____.

Do I Know It Now?

6 **Think about it.**

A. Go to page 78. Look and circle again.

B. Check (✔).

☐ I can start the next unit.

☐ I can ask my teacher for help and then start the next unit.

☐ I can practice and then start the next unit.

7 **Rate this Checkpoint. Color the stars.**

easy   hard   fun   not fun

Checkpoint Units 4–6   81

unit 7
Party Time

1 Listen and read. Then sing.

My Birthday Party

Welcome, friends.
Please sit down.
It's my birthday party!
With games and a clown!

We have pizza, hot dogs,
Salad, too.
Apples, cake,
And ice cream for you!

Or put a hamburger
On your plate.
With juice or milk
It'll taste great.

Thanks for the presents.
What a great day!
Let's eat and drink
And play, play, play.

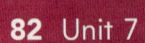

2 Listen. Point and say.

1. an apple
2. an orange
3. grapes
4. salad
5. a hot dog
6. a hamburger
7. a sandwich
8. pizza
9. cake
10. ice cream
11. milk
12. juice

3 Listen and say. Write.

1. She's eating _____.
2. He's drinking _____. 
3. They're eating _____. 
4. She's drinking _____. 
5. He's eating a _____. 
6. They're eating _____. 

4 Look at 3. Listen. Ask and answer with a partner.

What's she eating?

She's eating grapes.

Unit 7

Story

🎧 **5** Listen to the story.

How Many More Days?

1. My birthday! My birthday! My birthday's coming!

2. When's your birthday, Max? — My birthday's on Saturday! Just *four* more days!

3. What day is today? — Today is Monday.

MARCH
SUNDAY	MONDAY	TUESDAY	WEDNESDAY	THURSDAY	FRIDAY	SATURDAY
1	2	3	4	5	6	7 🎉
8	9	10	11	12	13	14
15	16	17	18	19	20	21
22	23	24	25	26	27	28
29	30	31				

4. So, Tuesday, Wednesday, Thursday, Friday, then Saturday! — Oh, no! That's *five* more days!

84 Unit 7

> That's just one more than four. It's not long.

> OK. Just *five* more days! Then it's my birthday!

5

6

6 Look at the story. When is Max's birthday? Circle the day and color the picture.

SUNDAY MONDAY
TUESDAY WEDNESDAY
THURSDAY FRIDAY
SATURDAY

7 THINK BIG **Write.**

1. There are _____ days in one week.

2. Today is _____.

Language in Action

8 **Listen and read. Say.**

Tom: What do you have, Ben?
Ben: I have a present for you. Happy birthday, Tom!
Tom: Thanks!
Ben: Is Matt here?
Tom: Yes, he is.
Ben: Oh, good. He has a great present for you!

9 **Work with a partner. Look at 8. Role-play.**

10 **Listen. Stick.**

Grammar

> What **does** he **have**? He **has** milk.
> What **do** you **have**? I **have** juice.

11 Listen and circle.

1.
2.
3.
4.

12 Look at **11**. Ask and answer with a partner.

What does she have?

She has cake and milk.

Unit 7

Connections | Content: Science

13 Look. Listen and say.

1. Wow! It's hot!
2. Brrr! It's cold!

14 Listen and match.

COLD   HOT

15 Draw one hot food and one cold food you like.

88 Unit 7

Around the World | **Connections**

16 Look. Listen and say.

Birthday Fun

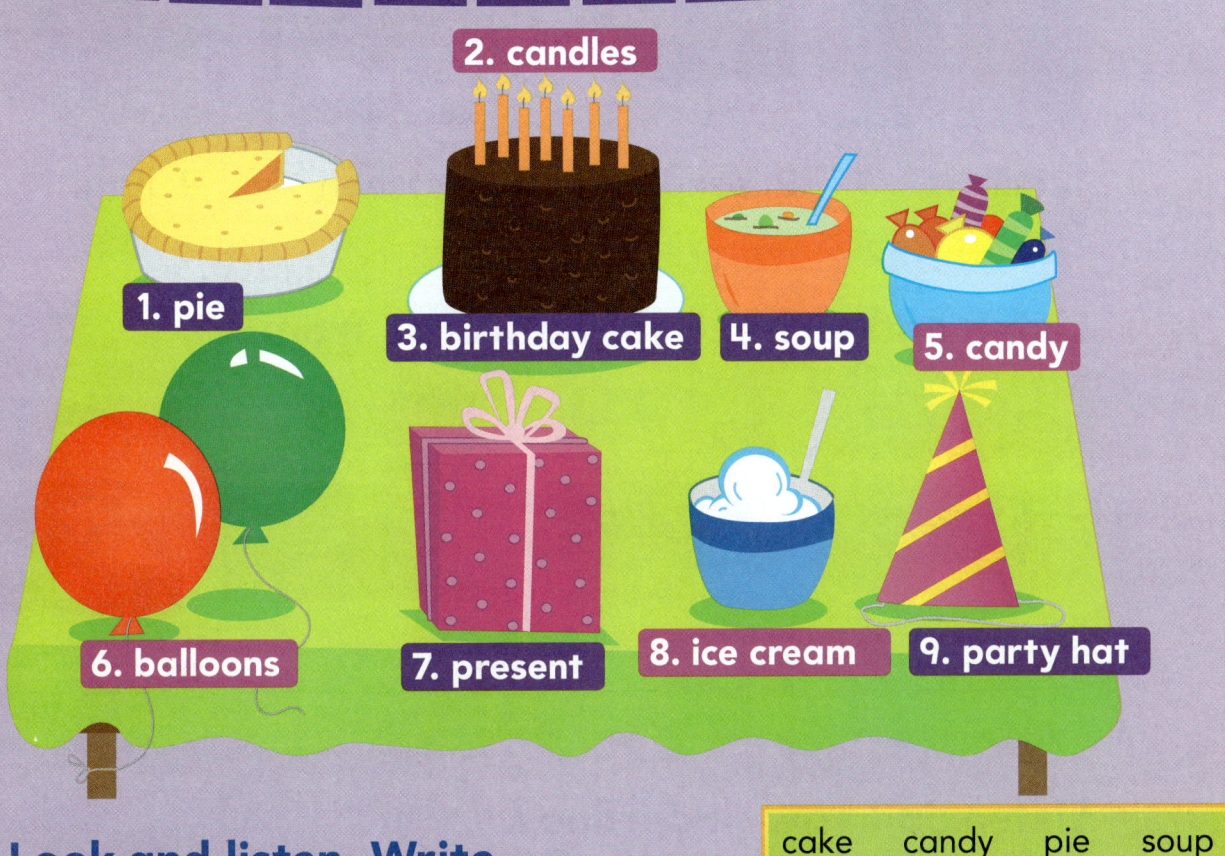

1. pie
2. candles
3. birthday cake
4. soup
5. candy
6. balloons
7. present
8. ice cream
9. party hat

| cake | candy | pie | soup |

17 Look and listen. Write.

Mexico　　United States　　Korea　　Russia

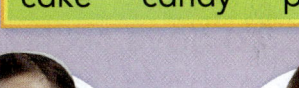

1. _____ 2. _____ 3. _____ 4. _____

18 Write about you.

My name is _____. On my birthday, I have _____, _____, and _____.

Unit 7 **89**

Sounds and Letters | Short *i* Sound

19. Listen. Point and say.

1. m**i**lk
2. sandw**i**ch
3. k**i**tchen
4. l**i**ttle

20. Listen and write. Use the words from 19.

1. _____
2. _____
3. _____
4. _____

21. Listen and say. Underline *i*.

1. We have six little chicks on the farm.
2. Tim is swimming in the pool.
3. Chris and Mindy drink milk from pink glasses.
4. Sit here and listen to this music.

Celebrate. | **Values in Action**

22 **Listen. Find and number.**

Birthday   Father's Day    New Year's Day

23 **Look at 22. Role-play with a partner.**

Happy New Year!

Thank you. Happy New Year to you!

PROJECT

24 **Make a Greeting Card.**

1. Fold. **2.** Write. **3.** Cut. **4.** Paste. **5.** Color.

Review | Listening and Speaking

25 **Look at Picture A and Picture B. Find four differences. Talk with a partner.**

Picture A

Picture B

In Picture A, the cake has seven candles.

In Picture B, the cake has one candle.

92 Unit 7

Vocabulary and Grammar | Review

26 **Look and match.**

Monday	Tuesday	Wednesday	Thursday	Friday	Saturday	Sunday
salad	hamburger	hot dog	grapes	pizza	cake	apple

1. On Monday, I have   a. cake.
2. On Tuesday, I have   b. pizza.
3. On Wednesday, I have   c. salad.
4. On Thursday, I have   d. a hamburger.
5. On Friday, I have   e. an apple.
6. On Saturday, I have   f. a hot dog.
7. On Sunday, I have   g. grapes.

27 **Look and write. Use *have* or *has*.**

1. They _____ a soccer ball.

2. She _____ birthday presents.

3. My sister _____ a blue bicycle.

4. My mother and father _____ a red car.

I Can
- ☐ talk about food and celebrations.
- ☐ say the days of the week.

Unit 7 93

Unit 8 Fun and Games

1 Listen and read. Then sing.

Please Put Your Toys Away

Mom, where's my action figure?
I've looked everywhere.
It's under the big blue chair.
What's it doing there?

Mom, I can't find my skates.
Do you know where they are?
Yes, yes, I think I do.
You left them in the car.

Mom, where's my airplane?
It's not on my shelf.
Try the toy box in your room.
Please look for it yourself!

Stop asking, "Where are my toys?"
And please do what I say.
After you're finished playing,
Please put your toys away!

2 Listen. Point and say.

1. action figure
2. airplane
3. ball
4. bike
5. blocks
6. cars
7. stuffed animal
8. doll
9. game
10. puppet
11. skates
12. train

3 Look. Listen and write.

1. I want _____.
2. I want a _____. 
3. I want an _____. 
4. I want a _____. 
5. I want a _____. 
6. I want a _____. 

4 Look at 2. Listen. Ask and answer with a partner.

What do you want?

I want an action figure.

Unit 8 **95**

Story

5. Listen to the story.

I Want My Toys

1. I want my skates, Daddy!
Sorry, Lizzie. No skating today. It's raining.

2. I want my bike, Daddy.
Sorry! No riding your bike in the living room.

3. Daddy, where's my doll?
It's under the sofa, Lizzie.

4. Oh, where are my action figures?

> Here they are. They're on the sofa.

> What are you doing, Lizzie?

> I'm playing with my friends!

5

6

6 Look at the story. Listen and circle.

1. Lizzie wants her 🛼 / 🔴 .

2. Lizzie's doll is under the 🪑 / 🟡 .

3. Lizzie is playing with her 🧑‍🤝‍🧑 / 🚲 .

7 Draw your favorite toy.

Unit 8 **97**

Language in Action

8 **Listen and say.**

Dan: Mom, where's my airplane?
Mom: It's under the table.
Dan: Oh, and where are my skates?
Mom: They're on the shelf.
Dan: Thanks. Where's my stuffed animal?
Mom: It's in the washing machine!

9 **Work with a partner. Look at 8. Role-play.**

10 **Listen. Stick.**

Grammar

Where's the ball? It's **in** the toy box.
It's **on** the shelf.
It's **under** the table.

Where are the skates? They're **under** the desk.
They're **on** the sofa.

11 Listen and check (✔).

1.

2.

3.

4.

12 Look at **11**. Ask and answer with a partner.

Where's the doll?

It's on the shelf.

Unit 8 **99**

Connections | Content: Math

13 Listen and trace. Point and say.

11	12	13	14	15
eleven	twelve	thirteen	fourteen	fifteen
16	17	18	19	20
sixteen	seventeen	eighteen	nineteen	twenty

14 Count the apples and write the number.

15 How old are you? Write the number. Draw the same number of apples in the box.

Apples

Around the World | Connections

16 Look and listen. Number.

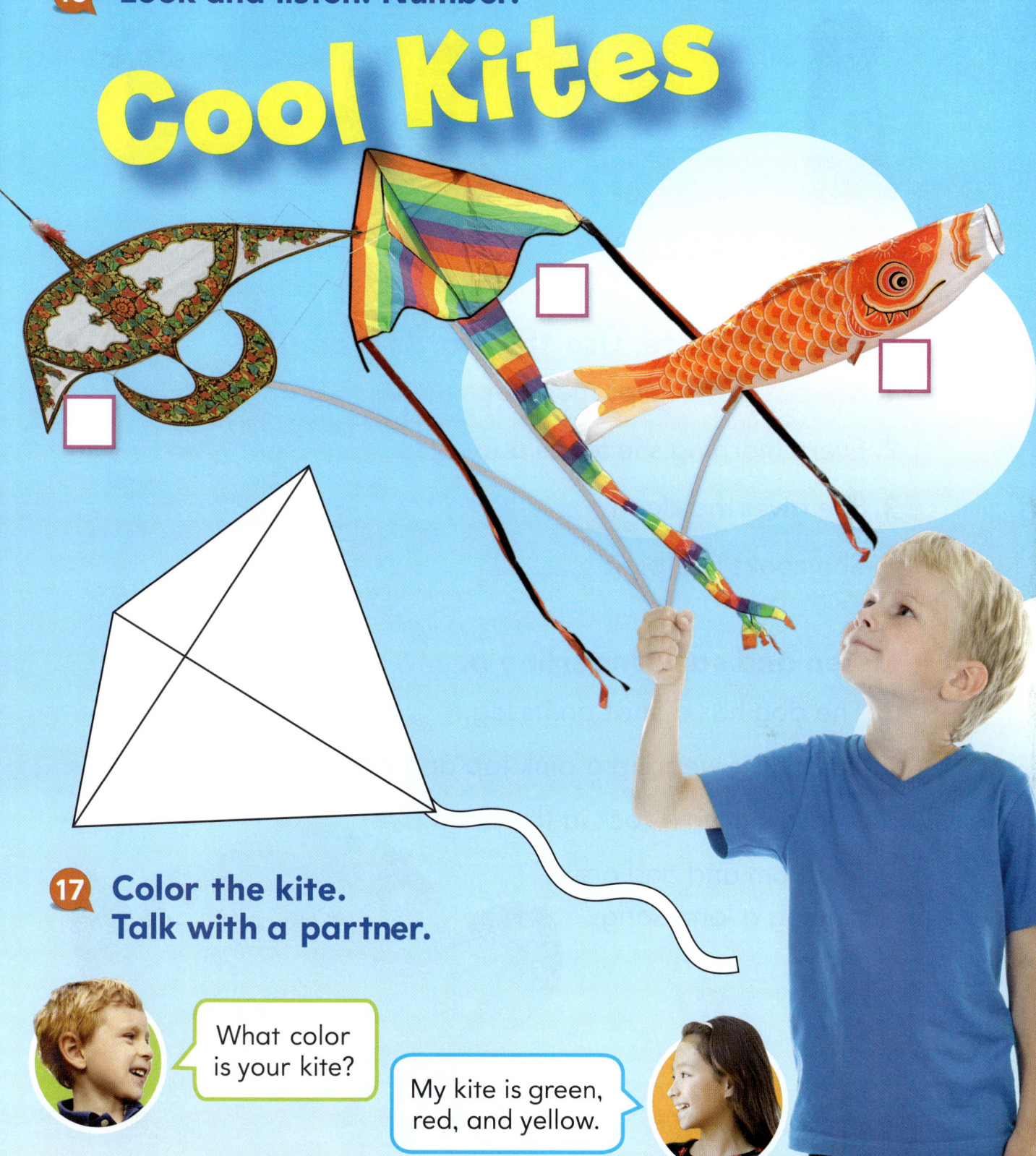

Cool Kites

17 Color the kite.
Talk with a partner.

What color is your kite?

My kite is green, red, and yellow.

18 THINK BIG Why do people from all over the world like kites?

Sounds and Letters | Short o Sound

19 Listen and point. Say.

1. dog
2. pot
3. socks
4. mom

20 Listen and write. Use the words from 19.

1. My _____ helps me a lot.

2. Every morning she feeds our _____.

3. She gives me clean _____.

4. She cooks in a big _____.

21 Listen and say. Underline o.

1. The dog has a spot on its leg.

2. The doll is wearing a pink top and white socks.

3. A frog sits on a rock in the pond.

4. My mom and dad are singing a long song.

Share your toys. | **Values in Action**

22 **Listen. Number in order.**

☐ ☐ ☐

23 **How do you share with your friends? Act it out with a partner.**

Here's my airplane. Let's share.

OK. Thank you!

PROJECT

24 **Make a Fun Kite to show and share.**

1. Draw.  **2.** Cut.  **3.** Paste.  **4.** Show.

Review | Listening and Speaking

25 **Look. Count and write. Listen and check.**

1. _2_ airplanes   2. ___ stuffed animals   3. ___ balls
4. ___ skates   5. ___ action figures   6. ___ dolls

26 **Look at 25. Ask and answer with a partner.**

How many airplanes do you see?

I see two airplanes.

Where are they?

One airplane is on the shelf. One is under the desk.

Vocabulary and Grammar | Review

27 **Look and write.**

1. Where's my _____?

2. Do you like my new _____?

3. I want a big _____.

4. Look at my _____.

5. That's a funny _____.

6. Let's play a _____.

airplane
bike
doll
game
puppet
train

28 **Look and write *in*, *on*, or *under*.**

1. They're _____ the table.

2. It's _____ the toy box.

3. It's _____ the chair.

I Can
- ☐ tell where something is.
- ☐ say what I want.
- ☐ count from 11 to 20.

Unit 8 **105**

unit 9 Play Time

1 Listen and read. Then sing.

Play Time Is Cool!

We like play time at our school.
Jumping and dancing,
Throwing and catching.
Play time is cool at our school!

I'm throwing the ball.
It's so much fun!
She's hitting. He's catching.
Let's get a home run!

We're playing soccer.
And we need to score
A goal! It's 2 to 1!
Let's get two more.

2 Listen. Point and say.

1. catching
2. throwing
3. hitting
4. kicking
5. jumping
6. dancing
7. singing
8. skating
9. riding
10. running

3 Listen and say.

1. **This** ball is green.
2. **That** ball is orange.
3. **These** skates are blue.
4. **Those** skates are red.

4 Look around your classroom. Listen to the model. Talk with a partner about what you see.

This table is big.

These chairs are brown.

Unit 9

Story

5 Listen to the story.

I'm Not Tired!

1
- Hi, Ann.
- Hi, Mrs. Ramos.

2
- Thanks for babysitting, Ann. Is Jimmy sleeping?
- No, he isn't, Mrs. Ramos.

3
- What's he doing?
- He's jumping on his bed.

4
- It's time to go to sleep, Jimmy.
- I'm not tired! I'm not tired!

What's he doing now?

He's dancing.

It's quiet! Is he sleeping?

Yes, he's sleeping now!

6   **Look at the story. Number the pictures in order.**

7   **THINK BIG What about you? Write.**

I like _____

_____

dancing
jumping
running
singing
throwing

Unit 9   109

Language in Action

8. Listen and say.

Dad: Where's Amy?
Tim: She's going to school.
Dad: Is she riding her bike?
Tim: No, she isn't.
Dad: Is she taking the bus?
Tim: No, she isn't. She's skating!

9. Work with a partner. Look at 8. Role-play.

10. Listen. Stick.

Grammar

Is she **singing**?	Yes, she **is**.	No, she **isn't**.
Are they **dancing**?	Yes, they **are**.	No, they **aren't**.

B58

11 Listen and number.

12 Look at **11**. Ask and answer with a partner.

Is he running?

No, he isn't. He's riding a bike.

Unit 9

Connections | Content: Physical Education

13. Listen and say. Write.

clap   dance   fly   jump   sit   turn

1. _____
2. _____
3. _____
4. _____
5. _____
6. _____

14. Listen. Then chant and do the actions!

Clap Your Hands

Clap, clap. Clap your hands!
Come on and clap with me.
Now jump, jump. Jump up high!
Come on. Give it one more try.
Now flap your arms. Fly, fly, fly.
Try and reach up to the sky.
Now dance, dance. Dance with me.
Come on. It's not hard. It's easy.
Now it's time to turn around.
Whew! I'm tired! Let's sit down!

Around the World | Connections

15 Look and listen.

Rock, Paper, Scissors

1. Canada
2. Japan
3. Chile

16 Look and listen. Say and do the action.

1. rock
2. paper 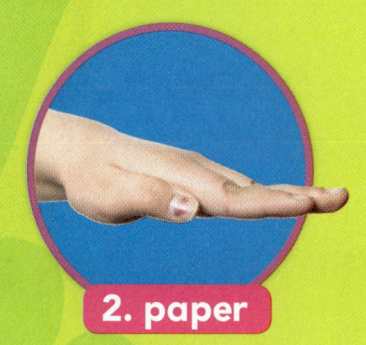
3. scissors 

17 Look, listen, and say. Play with a friend.

1. Rock breaks scissors. Rock wins!
2. Scissors cut paper. Scissors win!
3. Paper covers rock. Paper wins!

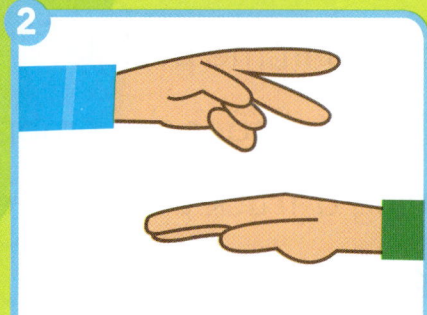

Unit 9 113

Sounds and Letters | Short *u* Sound

18 **Listen. Point and say.**

1. f**u**n
2. r**u**n
3. j**u**mp
4. l**u**nch

19 **Listen and write. Use the words from 18.**

1. At our school, play time is after _____.
2. Some kids _____ in the school yard.
3. Other kids _____ rope or play ball.
4. Play time is always _____.

20 **Listen and say. Underline *u*.**

1. The duck is jumping in the puddle.
2. The stuffed animal is under the umbrella.
3. My uncle is driving a truck up the street.
4. The funny puppet is playing a drum.

Take care of your body. | Values in Action

21 Look and listen. Then write.

jumping
kicking
running

1. _____   2. _____   3. _____

22 Ask and answer with a partner. Act it out.

What are you doing?

I'm jumping.

PROJECT

23 Make a **Daily Exercise** chart to show and share.

	S	M	T	W	T	F	S
Jump	5 min						
Kick	5 min						
Run	10 min						

Unit 9　115

Review | Listening and Speaking

24 **Listen and circle.**

25 **Look at the picture in 24. Ask and answer with a partner. Use all the action words.**

catching
eating
flying
jumping
running
singing
skating
swimming
throwing

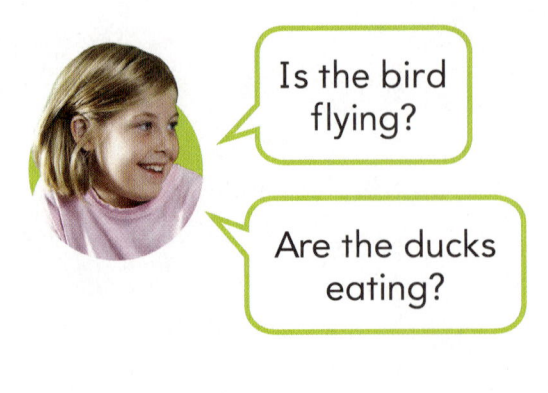

Is the bird flying?

Are the ducks eating?

Yes, it is.

No, they aren't. They're swimming.

Vocabulary and Grammar | Review

26 Listen and number.

27 Look and write.

That
These
This
Those

1. _____ boots are old.

2. _____ dog is small.

3. _____ sandwich is big.

4. _____ pencils are yellow.

I Can
☐ talk about and do actions.
☐ take care of my body.

Unit 9 117

Checkpoint | Units 7–9

Do I Know It?

1. **Look and circle. Practice.**

   😊 I know this.   😕 I don't know this.

1. p. 83	**2.** pp. 84–85
3. p. 95	**4.** p. 100
5. p. 107	**6.** p. 107 — these, those

   Have students review the key language. Go to the pages indicated in each box.

   118 Checkpoint Units 7–9

I Can Do It!

2 Get ready.

A. Look. Listen to the questions. Circle the correct words.

1. It's on the **shelf / table**.
2. They're **on / under** the bed.
3. Yes, **he / she** does.

B. Listen again and check. Then practice with a partner.

C. Look at **A**. Answer these questions with a partner.
1. What foods do you see? What drinks do you see?
2. How many toys do you see? What are they?
3. What day is it?

Checkpoint Units 7–9

Checkpoint | Units 7–9

3 **Get set.**

STEP 1 Cut out the outline on page 127.

STEP 2 Fold the paper to make a book.

STEP 3 Write in your book. Color the cake.
Now you're ready to **Go!**

4 **Go!**

A. Read your book with three classmates. Take turns.
Write the presents.

Classmate	Present
Bruno	a train set
1	
2	
3	

B. Look at your books. Answer these questions with a partner.

1. Page 2: What are they doing?

2. Page 3: What foods do they have?

3. Page 3: Where's the cat?

4. Page 4: How many presents do you see?

5 **Write or draw.**

All About Me

My favorite food is
_____.

My favorite toy is
_____.

Do I Know It Now?

6 **Think about it.**

A. Go to page 118. Look and circle again.

B. Check (✔).

☐ I can ask my teacher for help.
☐ I can practice.

7 **Rate this Checkpoint. Color the stars.**

☆ easy   ☆ hard | ☆ fun   ☆ not fun

Checkpoint Units 7–9

Cutouts for Page 40, Checkpoint Units 1–3

Checkpoint Cutouts Units 1–3

Cutouts for Page 80, Checkpoint Units 4–6

Checkpoint Cutouts Units 4–6

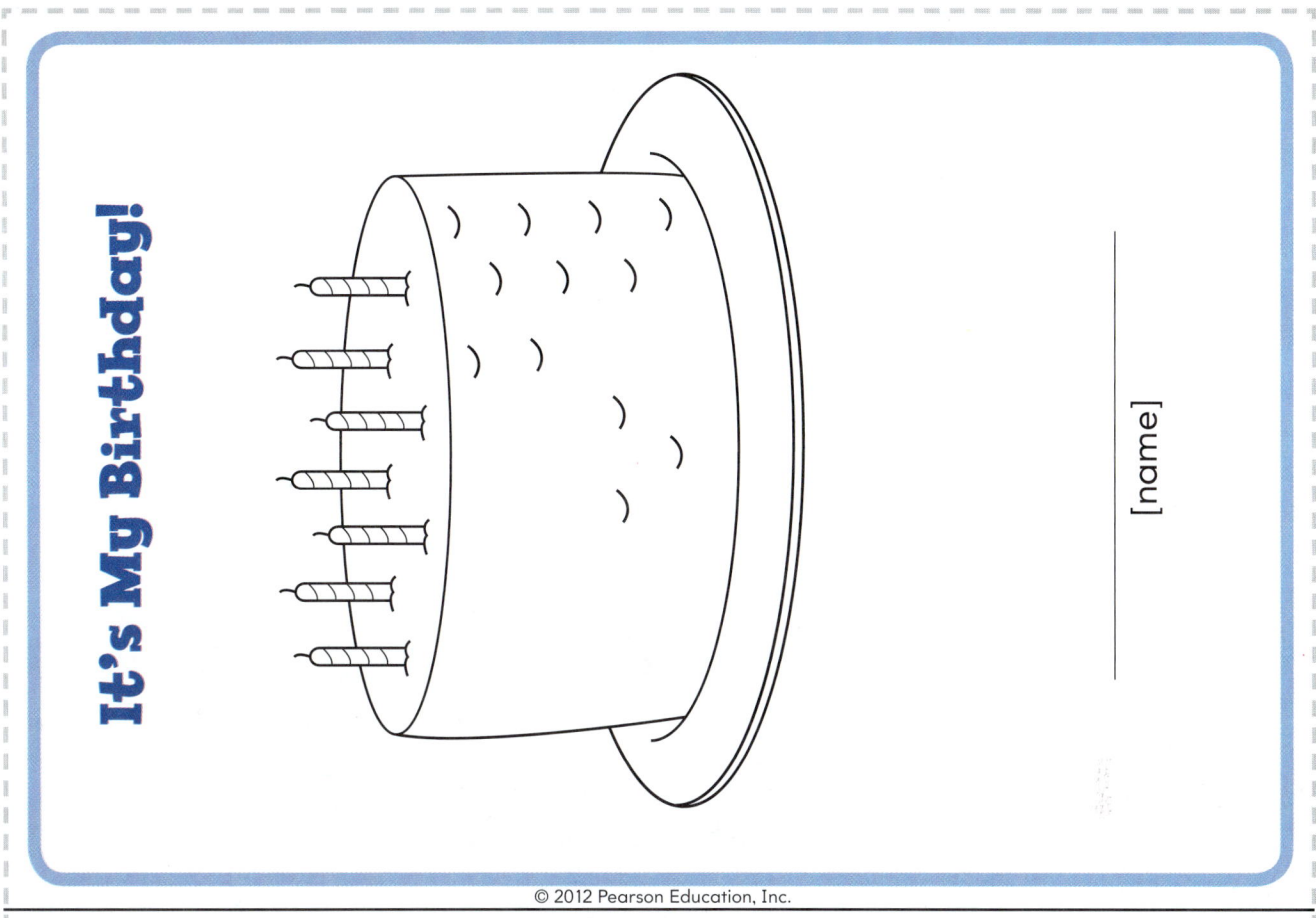

Cutouts for Page 120, Checkpoint Units 7–9

It's My Birthday!

_____
[name]

© 2012 Pearson Education, Inc.

I have a present. It's a _____ .
[toy]
I'm happy today!

4

Checkpoint Cutouts Units 7–9 127

Cutouts for Page 120, Checkpoint Units 7–9

Today is _____ [day].

It's my birthday! I'm having a party.

2

My friends are eating _____ [food].

3

Young Learners English
Starters

Practice Materials
Sampler

Note to students:
These practice materials will help you prepare for the YLE (Young Learners English) Tests. There are three kinds of tests in this sampler: Listening, Reading & Writing, and Speaking. Good luck!

Listening A

– 5 questions –

Look at the picture. Now listen and look. There is one example.

130 Listening A

Listening B

– 5 questions –

Look at the pictures. Now listen and look. There is one example.

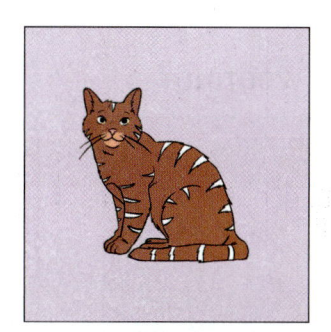

Listening C

– 5 questions –

Look at the pictures. Now listen and look. There is one example.

What's she wearing?

A  ✓   B  ☐   C ☐

1 Where is he?

A  ☐   B  ☐   C ☐

2 What's she doing?

A  ☐   B  ☐   C ☐

132 Listening C

3   What are they?

A  ☐   B  ☐   C ☐

4   What are the cats doing?

A  ☐   B  ☐   C ☐

5   What are his favorite clothes?

A  ☐   B  ☐   C ☐

Listening C 133

Reading & Writing A

– 5 questions –

Look and read. Put a check (✓) or an (✗) in the box.
There are two examples.

Examples

This is a chair. ✓

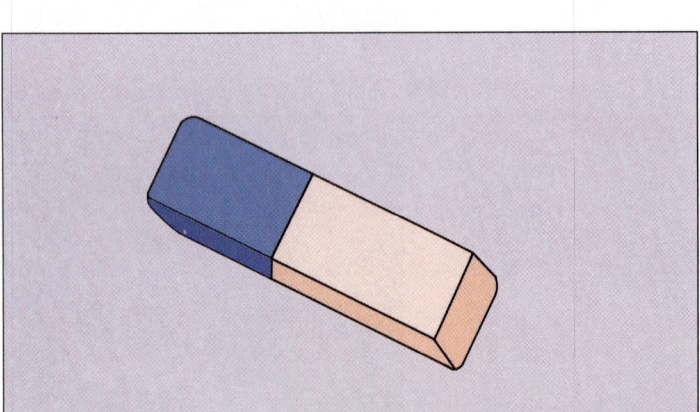

This is a ruler. ✗

Questions

1

This is a baby. ☐

2

This is a foot. ☐

3

This is a book. ☐

4

This is a sister. ☐

5

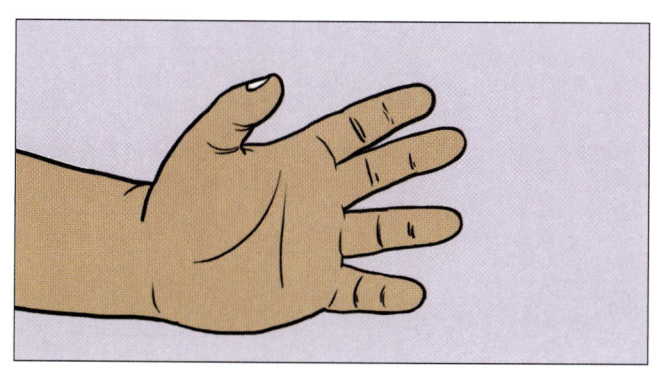

This is a hand. ☐

Reading & Writing B

– 5 questions –

Look and read. Write *yes* or *no*.

Examples

The farmer is wearing boots.	yes
The dog is running.	no

Questions

1 The girl is feeding the ducks. _____

2 The chickens are eating. _____

3 The girl has short hair. _____

4 The boy is reading a book. _____

5 The farmer has a red shirt. _____

Reading & Writing C

– 5 questions –

Look at the pictures. Look at the letters. Write the words.

Example

<u>t</u> <u>r</u> <u>a</u> <u>i</u> <u>n</u>   a r n t i

Questions

1. _ _ _ _ _ _   g n a o e r

2. _ _ _ _ _ _   t p u p e p

3. _ _ _ _ _   l a d s a

4. _ _ _ _ _ _   t a k s e s

5. _ _ _ _ _ _ _ _   d i n s h c a w

Speaking A

138 Speaking A

Speaking B

Speaking C

Photo credits: Page i (l) Brand New Images/Lifesize/Getty Images; (lc) Michaeljung/Shutterstock; (c) Digital Media Pro/Shutterstock; (rc) Anatoliy Samara/Shutterstock; (r) Keren Su/China Span/Getty Images; (bkg) Vitezslav Valka/Shutterstock ; iii (bee) Andrey Armyagov/Shutterstock; 2 (bl) Darrin Henry/Shutterstock, (br) Darrin Henry/Shutterstock, (tcl) Gelpi/Shutterstock, (tcr) Anatoliy Samara/Shutterstock; 3 (tl) Eurobanks/Dreamstime, (tcl) Nikshor/Dreamstime, (tc) Py2000/Dreamstime, (tcr) Lucie Lang/Shutterstock, (tr) Kjpargeter/Dreamstime, (cl eraser) Phartisan/Dreamstime, (cl marker) Ingvar Bjork/Shutterstock, (c) Fibobjects/Dreamstime, (cr pencil) Cphoto/Dreamstime, (cr ruler) karen roach/Dreamstime, (bl) SergiyN/Shutterstock, (br) SergiyN/Shutterstock; 6 (tr) Dmitriy Shironosov/Shutterstock; 7 (br) SergiyN/Shutterstock, (bl) SergiyN/Shutterstock; 8 (t) Mushakesa/Shutterstock, (br) Lucie Lang/Shutterstock; 9 (bkgd) gabor210/Shutterstock, (tc) Insy Shah/AGE Fotostock, (tr) Datacraft/AGE Fotostock, (tl) Rmarmion/Dreamstime, (br) SergiyN/Shutterstock, (bl) SergiyN/Shutterstock, (c) Cphoto/Dreamstime, (br) Cphoto/Dreamstime; 10 (bl) SergiyN /Shutterstock, (br) SergiyN/Shutterstock; 11 (br) Effe45/Dreamstime; 13 (cr) Kingjon/Dreamstime, (b) Aeolos/Dreamstime, (tcr) Margaret M Stewart/Shutterstock, (tr) Lucie Lang/Shutterstock, (cl) kropic1/Shutterstock; 14 (bl) kuttelvaserova/Shutterstock, (br) Yuri Arcurs/Shutterstock; 15 (t) Shutterstock, (br) Corbis Cusp/Alamy, (bl) UpperCut Images/Alamy, (inset) Andresr/Shutterstock; 18 (tr) Darrinhenry/Dreamstime; 19 (tl) Iofoto/Dreamstime, (tc) Andreaslatter/Dreamstime, (bcr) MaszaS/Getty Images, (c) Shutterstock, (cl) Iofoto/Dreamstime, (tcr) Phartisan/Dreamstime, (cr) Maszas/Dreamstime, (tr) Yuri Arcurs/Shutterstock, (br) Corbis Cusp/Alamy, (bl) UpperCut Images/Alamy; 20 (tr) Isselee/Dreamstime, (cl) Bazil8/Dreamstime, (cr) Vaida/Shutterstock, (tl) Isselee/Dreamstime; 21 (l) Mark Yuill/Shutterstock, (br) juan carlos tinjaca/Shutterstock; 22 (tl) Websubstance/Dreamstime, (tcl) Lisovskaya Natalia/Shutterstock, (tr) Yuri_arcurs/Dreamstime, (tcr) Macniak/Dreamstime, (c ball) Chromorange/Dreamstime, (c box) Akiwi61/Dreamstime, (cr) Bear66/Dreamstime, (cl) Pearljamfan75/Dreamstime; 24 (b) discpicture/Shutterstock; 25 (tr) PtImages2/Dreamstime, (c kidsorange) VojtechVlk/Shutterstock, (cr) Sonyae/Dreamstime, (tcl) Tobkatrina/Dreamstime, (tcr) Darrin Henry/Shutterstock, (tl) Teraberb/Dreamstime, (c boys) Gigule/Dreamstime, (cl) Teraberb/Dreamstime, (bl) Shutterstock, (br) michaeljung/Shutterstock, (bc) Shutterstock; 26 (b) Valeriy Lebedev/Shutterstock, (tr) pzAxe/iStockphoto; 27 (l) Yuri Arcurs/Shutterstock, (br) Andy Dean/Fotolia, (bl) Fancy/Alamy; 30 (tr) Jeff Greenough/Blend Images/Alamy, (tcr) kedrov/Shutterstock, (b) Pichugin Dmitry/Shutterstock; 31 (tcl) rubberball/AGEfotostock, (tcr) Raycan/Dreamstime, (cl) Perrush/Dreamstime, (c dog) Sparkmom/Dreamstime, (tl) Alexander Raths/Shutterstock, (c man) Yuri Arcurs/Shutterstock, (cr) PT Images/Shutterstock, (tl) East/Shutterstock, (tcr) Raycan/Dreamstime, (bl) Fancy/Alamy, (br) Andy Dean/Fotolia; 32 (tcl) Armonn/Dreamstime, (tcr) Pressmaster/Dreamstime, (c sky) Happy person/Shutterstock, (c rose) San32/Dreamstime, (bc) Blueee/Dreamstime, (c guitar) Bear66/Dreamstime, (tl) Mayangsari/Dreamstime, (tr) jjshaw14/iStockphoto, (br) Kisialiou Yury/Shutterstock; 33 (cl) Jürgen Priewe/Fotolia, (c) Jürgen Priewe/Fotolia, (bcr) Fancy/Alamy, (br) Andy Dean/Fotolia, (cr) AntonSokolov/Shutterstock; 34 (tcl) Ginosphotos/Dreamstime, (tl) ayzek/Shutterstock, (tcr) Valua Vitaly/Shutterstock, (cl) Morena Valente/Shutterstock, (c bat) Germany Feng/Shutterstock, (c dog) Eriklam/Dreamstime, (tr) Gravicapa/iStockphoto, (cr) ozgurdonmaz/iStockphoto; 36 (bl) Fancy/Alamy, (br) Andy Dean/Fotolia; 37 (tcl) Eriklam/Dreamstime, (tcr) chatursunil/Shutterstock, (cl) swissmacky/Shutterstock, (tl) Pavelshlykov/Dreamstime, (cgirl) Justmeyo/Dreamstime, (tr) Oxilixo/Dreamstime, (bcl) Gorbelabda/Dreamstime, (bcr) Ilya Andriyanov/Shutterstock, (br)Stephanie Frey/Dreamstime, (bl) Ninell/Dreamstime, (cbird) Zugzwang/Dreamstime, (cr) itsallgood/Fotolia; 38 (tl) 3103/Shutterstock, (tl) Lucie Lang/Shutterstock, (tl) Phartisan/Dreamstime, (cr) Yuri Arcurs/Shutterstock, (bl) Yuri Arcurs/Shutterstock, (br) Perrush/Dreamstime, (br) Sparkmom/Dreamstime; 41 (br) wacpan/Shutterstock; 42 (l) Anatoliy Samara/Shutterstock, (br) michaeljung/Shutterstock; 43 (tl) Pavel V Mukhin/Shutterstock, (tcl) Semen Lihodeev/Alamy, (tc) ppfoto13/Shutterstock, (tcr) mustafacan/Dreamstime, (tr) Karkas/Shutterstock, (clshirt) Kalina Vova/Dreamstime, (clpants) largeformat4x5/iStockphoto, (cr) PhotoNAN/Shutterstock, (c) karkas/Shutterstock, (bcr legs) Forster Forest/Shutterstock, (bcr child) photoeuphoria/Dreamstime, (bcr girl) 3bugsmom/iStockphoto, (bcr yellowgirl) Steve Shott (c) Dorling Kindersley/dkImages, (bl) SergiyN/Shutterstock, (br) SergiyN/Shutterstock; 47 (bl) zoomstudio/iStockphoto, (br) SergiyN/Shutterstock; 48 (bc) Agap13/Dreamstime, (bl) Aliaksei Lasevich/Shutterstock, (bcl mountain) Goinyk/Dreamstime, (tr) Volodymyr Goinyk/Shutterstock, (tr) NHPA/SuperStock, (c) Lilu2005/Shutterstock, (bcl girl) Roijoy/Fotolia, (cl) Bannerx/Dreamstime; 49 (tr) Alastair Grant/APWideWorld, (cr) Taiga/Shutterstock, (c) Chas/Shutterstock, (tc) MICHAEL WEBBERLEY/Newscom, (cl) Rob Hainer/Shutterstock, (tl) David Wimsett/Newscom, (br) Tassh/Shutterstock, (bl) SergiyN/Shutterstock, (bc) SergiyN/Shutterstock; 50 (clgirl) Goldenkb/Dreamstime, (clhat) Eholmes5 / Dreamstime, (cr) Oleksiy Maksymenko Photography/Alamy, (tr) Eric Isselée/Shutterstock, (tl) Artmim/Shutterstock, (c) D900/Dreamstime, (tcl) Alexander Dashewsky/Shutterstock; 51 (tl) DU BOISBERRANGER Jean/AGE Fotostock, (tc) JTB Photo Communications, Inc./Alamy, (tr) SuperStock/AGE Fotostock, (b) siamionau pavel/Shutterstock, (cl) SergiyN/Shutterstock, (cr) SergiyN/Shutterstock; 53 (bl) greenland/Shutterstock, (bcl) Roman Sigaev/Shutterstock, (bcr) Olga Popova/Shutterstock, (br) Windujedi/Dreamstime; 54 (bl) Peter Cade/Getty Images, (br) Kraig Scarbinsky/Getty Images, (cr) Susanna Price/Getty Images; 55 (bl) SergiyN/Shutterstock, (br) SergiyN/Shutterstock; 58 (tr) Pascal Broze/Getty Images; 59 (tl) Peter Dazeley/Getty Images, (tcl) StockLite/Shutterstock, (tcr) Gyorgy Barna/Shutterstock, (tr) Ryan McVay/Getty Images, (cl) Sophia Vourdoukis/Getty Images, (c boy) Chris Amaral /Getty Images, (c girl) Gbh007/Dreamstime, (cr) Beto Hacker/Getty Images, (bl) SergiyN/Shutterstock, (br) SergiyN/Shutterstock; 60 (border tr) Graffiti/Shutterstock; 61 (tl) Jon Shireman/Getty Images, (tr) Bruno Morandi/Getty Images, (cl) Michael Matthews/Alamy, (cr) Stuart Monk/Shutterstock, (bl) SergiyN/Shutterstock, (bcl) SergiyN/Shutterstock; 62 (tl) Viktor1/Shutterstock, (tcl) Mike Flippo/Shutterstock, (tcr) wavebreakmedia ltd/Shutterstock, (tr) MAErtek/Shutterstock; 63 (tl) Wavebreak Media Ltd/123RF, (tr) kate_sept2004/iStockphoto; 65 (tl) Shutterstock, (tr) ChmpagnDave/Shutterstock, (tc) haveseen/Shutterstock, (cl) Vstock LLC/Getty Images, (cr) Andrea Chu/Getty Images, (bl) Ryzhov/Dreamstime, (bcl) Donna Alberico/Getty Images, (bcr) Fuse/Getty Images, (br) Paul Bradbury/Getty Images; 66 (tr) Eei_tony/Dreamstime, (br) AnetaPics/Shutterstock, (bcl) Eric Isselée/Shutterstock, (bl) Eric Isselée/Shutterstock, (b) Anna Sedneva/Shutterstock; 67 (tc cow) Martin Nemec/Shutterstock, (tcl duck) Ankevanwyk/Dreamstime, (tc frog) Kwasny221 /Dreamstime, (tcr goat) Rockywaters Tom Eagan/Dreamstime, (tcr chick) Tomas Sereda/Dreamstime, (tl horse) Alexeys/Dreamstime, (tl cat) spaxia/Dreamstime, (tcl dog) Valery Shklovskiy/Shutterstock, (tcr sheep) Randy Rimland/Shutterstock, (cl frog) Eduard Kyslynskyy/Shutterstock, (c sheep) H. Tuller/Shutterstock, (cr horse) Lenkadan/Shutterstock, (cl cow) Martin Nemec/Shutterstock, (c dog) Mike Tan C. T./Shutterstock, (cr duck) Michal Ninger/Shutterstock, (tr turtle) s-eyerkaufer/Shutterstock, (bl) Fancy/Alamy, (br) Andy Dean/Fotolia; 70 (tr) MBI/Alamy; 71 (bl) Fancy/Alamy, (br) Andy, Dean/Fotolia; 72 (tc) Anneka/Shutterstock, (tl) mathom/Shutterstock, (tr) mojito.mak[dog]gmail[dot]com/Shutterstock; 73 (cl) Shutterstock, (c) mamahoohooba/Shutterstock, (tl) BlankaB/Shutterstock, (cr) Goodynewshoes/Dreamstime, (tr) granata1111/Shutterstock, (tc) wavebreakmedia ltd/Shutterstock, (bl) Danolsen/Dreamstime, (bcr) Teerapun/Shutterstock, (bc) Clark Brennan/Alamy (b) Michael Pettigrew/Shutterstock; 74 (tr) Hintau Aliaksei/Shutterstock, (tcl) Valentina_S/Shutterstock, (tcr) Hintau Aliaksei/Shutterstock, (tl) 101cats/iStockphoto; 75 (tcr) Hybrid Images/AGE Fotostock, (tl) windzepher/Fotolia, (tcl) Golden Pixels LLC/Shutterstock, (tr) Ruth Black/AGE Fotostock, (cl) Fancy/Alamy, (c) Andy Dean/Fotolia; 76 (cl) Gelpi /Shutterstock, (cr) Petroruth/Dreamstime, (tr) Alkestida/Shutterstock, (c) Golden Pixels LLC/Shutterstock, (tl) Yuri_arcurs/Dreamstime, (bl) aabejon/iStockphoto, (br) nicolesy/iStockphoto; 77 (cl) AdventureStock/Shutterstock, (tl) Alucard2100/Dreamstime, (tr) djgis/Shutterstock, (tcr) Amaviael /Dreamstime, (cr) bimmergirl/Dreamstime, (tcl) Morgan Lane Photography/Shutterstock, (br) Jane McIlroy/Shutterstock, (bcl) Ankevanwyk/Dreamstime, (bcr) duoduo/Shutterstock, (bl) Anneka/Shutterstock; 78 (tl) TerraceStudio/Shutterstock, (tl) Pavel V Mukhin/Shutterstock, (tl) Maitree Laipitaksin/Shutterstock, (tr) zoomstudio/iStockphoto, (tr) SergiyN/Shutterstock.com, (cl) MarishaSha/Shutterstock, (cl) riana Shiyan/Shutterstock, (cr) Gyorgy Barna/Shutterstock, (cr) Beto Hacker/GettyImages, (bl) Alexeys/Dreamstime, (bl) Ankevanwyk/Dreamstime, (bl) Martin Nemec/Shutterstock, (br) Yuri arcurs/Dreamstime, (br) Alkestida/Shutterstock; 81 (br) wacpan/Shutterstock; 82 (br) Alexander Raths/Shutterstock, (bl) Arvind Balaraman/Shutterstock; 83 (tc sundae) karen roach/Shutterstock, (tcr milk) Horiyan/Shutterstock, (tcl sandwich) 3445128471/Shutterstock, (tcl pizza) Chris Bence/Shutterstock, (tc cake) James Steidl/Dreamstime, (tr hamburger) Leroy Harvey/Shutterstock, (tcr hotdog) Lane Erickson/Dreamstime, (tc salad) studio online/Shutterstock, (tc grapes) Peterzijlstra/Dreamstime, (tl apple) RimGlow/Dreamstime, (tcl orange) Midosemsem/Dreamstime, (bcr) ImAGE Source/AGE Fotostock, (cl) Joana Kruse/Shutterstock, (c) Shutterstock, (bcl) DenisNata/Shutterstock, (bc) Boris Mrdja/Shutterstock, (tcr juice) Nikreates/Alamy, (bl) Fancy/Alamy, (br) Andy Dean/Fotolia; 86 (tr) Thomas Northcut/Getty Images; 87 (bl) Fancy/Alamy, (br) Andy Dean/Fotolia; 88 (c) jcjgphotography/Shutterstock, (bcl) karen roach/Shutterstock, (bl) Leroy Harvey/Shutterstock, (cl) Brenda Carson/Dreamstime, (cr) Palle Christensen/Shutterstock, (bcr) Katstudio/Shutterstock, (br) M. Unal Ozmen/Shutterstock, (tl) Shebeko/Shutterstock, (tr) Valentyn Volkov/Shutterstock; 89 (bcl) Condor 36/Shutterstock, (br) Stephen Finn/Shutterstock, (bcr) Tetra Images/Alamy, (bl) Michelle D. Bridwell/Photo Edit; 90 (tl) Marius Graf/Fotolia, (tcr) Yauheni Krasnaok/Dreamstime, (tcl) kesu/Shutterstock, (tr) Murat Subatli/Shutterstock; 91 (tr) Eric Fahrner/Shutterstock, (tl) wavebreakmedia ltd/Shutterstock, (tc) Fuse/Getty Images, (cl) Fancy/Alamy, (cr) Andy Dean/Fotolia, (bl) Iwona Grodzka/Shutterstock, (br) Iwona Grodzka/Shutterstock; 92 (bl) Fancy/Alamy, (br) Andy Dean/Fotolia; 93 (tcl burger) Leroy Harvey/Shutterstock, (tc grapes) Aliaksandr Mazurkevich/Dreamstime, (tcrcake) Mau Horng/Shutterstock, (tl) ffolas/Shutterstock, (tcl hotdog) Aida Ricciardiello/Dreamstime, (tcr pizza) Stephen Mcsweeny/Dreamstime, (tr) ruigsantos/Dreamstime, (bcr) Andreas Gradin/Shutterstock, (bcl) Yurchyks/Shutterstock, (bl) Asia Images Group Pte Ltd/Alamy, (br) Jacek Chabraszewski/Dreamstime; 94 (tr) Nikolai Tsvetkov/Shutterstock, (cr) ladyminnie/iStockphoto, (bkgd) Vitalinka/Shutterstock, (br) Anke van Wyk/Shutterstock, (cl) Vitalik-sv/Dreamstime; 95 (tr) Icefields/Dreamstime, (tcl baby) Viktorfischer/Dreamstime, (tcl ball) Garry518/Dreamstime, (tcl game) Arbaes/Dreamstime, (tcr puppet) Sintez/Dreamstime, (tcr) Ladyminnie/Dreamstime, (tcr train) Ivonnewierink /Dreamstime, (tcl dog) Vykkdraygo/Dreamstime, (tcl plain) Milosluz/Dreamstime, (tc bike) Ia64/Dreamstime, (tl figure) Vitalik-sv/Dreamstime, (bcr) Arbaes/Dreamstime, (c) wacpan/Shutterstock, (bcl) Ivosar/Dreamstime, (cl) nito/Shutterstock, (cr) Margo Harrison/Shutterstock, (bl) Corbis Cusp/Alamy, (br) UpperCut Images/Alamy; 99 (bl) Corbis Cusp/Alamy, (br) UpperCut Images/Alamy; 101 (tc) R.V. Bulck/iStockphpoto, (tl) Afby71/Dreamstime, (tr) Akiyoko74/Dreamstime, (tcl) Jpsdg /Dreamstime, (tcl) Kitch Bain/Shutterstock, (bl) Corbis Cusp/Alamy, (br) UpperCut Images/Alamy; 102 (tl) Eric Isselée/Shutterstock, (tr) Nejron Photo/Shutterstock, (tcr) Aurinko/Dreamstime; 103 (bl) Corbis Cusp/Alamy, (br) UpperCut Images/Alamy; 104 (bl) Corbis Cusp/Alamy, (br) UpperCut Images/Alamy; 105 (airplane) Philcold/Dreamstime, (bike) Hamurishi/Dreamstime, (doll) Beepstock/Alamy, (train) Peter Dankov/Shutterstock, (puppet) Photka/Dreamstime, (boardgame) Tatik22/Shutterstock, (blocks) Jcjgphotography/Dreamstime, (toybox) Stephaniefrey/Dreamstime, (ball) Ronald Summers/Shutterstock, (chair) photosync/Shutterstock; 106 (bl) tan4ikk/Shutterstock, (tr) Jaimie Duplass/Shutterstock, (br) Digital Media Pro/Shutterstock; 107 (tl) Andreblais/Dreamstime, (cl dancer) Valeriylebedev/Dreamstime, (tc) Jeffwilliams87/Dreamstime, (tr) Cathy Yeulet/123RF, (tcr) Amy Myers/Shutterstock, (cr cyclist) Greenland/Dreamstime, (cr running kids) iofoto/Fotolia, (c) greenland/Shutterstock, (tcl) Supri Suharjoto/Shutterstock, (tl) Andreblais/Dreamstime, (tcl) Supri Suharjoto/Shutterstock, (tc) Jeffwilliams87/Dreamstime, (tcr) Amy Myers/Shutterstock, (tr) Cathy Yeulet/123RF, (cl) Valeriylebedev/Dreamstime, (cl child singing) Daren Baker/Dreamstime, (c) greenland/Shutterstock, (cr) Greenland/Dreamstime, (cr) iofoto/Fotolia, (bl) Fancy/Alamy, (br) Andy Dean/Fotolia; 111 (tl) greenland/Shutterstock, (bcr) paulaphoto/iStockphoto, (tr) Alon Othnay/Shutterstock, (c) wayrawayra/iStockphoto, (bcl) Sonyae/Dreamstime, (bc) Robert Daly/AGE Fotostock, (bl) Fancy/Alamy, (br) Andy Dean/Fotolia; 112 (tl) Gbh007/Dreamstime, (tr) Sofarina79/Shutterstock, (cr) Photo_Concepts/iStockphoto, (c) Vladimir Melnikov/Shutterstock, (bcl) Sonyae/Dreamstime, (tc) michaeljung/Shutterstock, (bcr) ZouZou/Shutterstock, (br) ZouZou/Shutterstock; 113 (tl) Anatoliy Samara/Shutterstock, (tc) xavierarnau/iStockphoto, (tr) sjlocke/iStockphoto, (c) dragon_fang/Shutterstock; 114 (cl) Cathy Yeulet/123RF, (tl) Anatoliy Samara/Shutterstock, (cr) Juice Images/AGE Fotostock, (tr) Shutterstock; 115 (tl) imAGE source/Fotolia, (tc) nicolesy/iStockphoto, (tr) Aflo Foto AGEncy/Alamy; 116 (bl) Fancy/Alamy, (br) Andy Dean/Fotolia; 117 (cl) Iakov Filimonov/Shutterstock, (tl) vnosokin/iStockphoto, (tr) Leah-Anne Thompson/Shutterstock, (tc) Aletia/Shutterstock, (c) Breck/Dreamstime, (cr) Alex Mares-Manton/Asia Images/Glow Images; 118 (tl) Leroy Harvey/Shutterstock, (tl) Peterzijlstra/Dreamstime, (tl) Nikreates / Alamy, (cl) Vitalik-sv/Dreamstime, (cl) Vykkdraygo/Dreamstime, (cl) Ladyminnie/Dreamstime, (bl) Breck/Dreamstime, (bl) Alex Mares-Manton/GlowImages, (br) ericlefrancais/Shutterstock, (br) Nadezda/Shutterstock; 121 (br) wacpan/Shutterstock.

Stickers

Unit 1, page 6

Unit 2, page 18

Unit 3, page 30

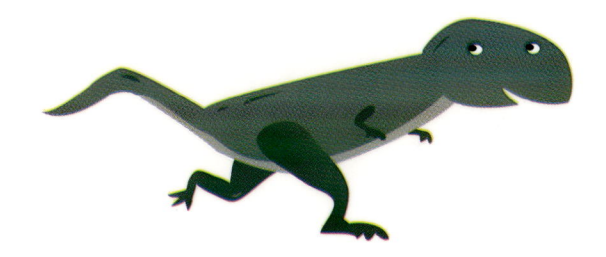

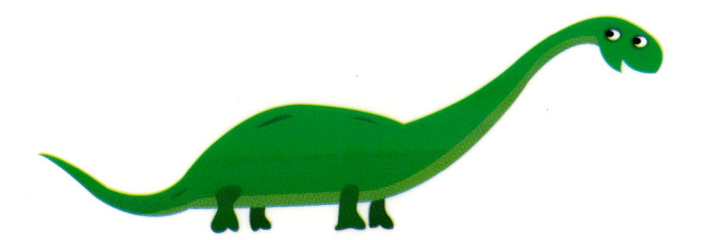

Stickers

Unit 4, page 46

Unit 5, page 58

Unit 6, page 70